"He

and deli

MW00617205

You Are

Already

Healed!!!

I pray that this book will be as much a blessing to you, the
reader, as it was for me to live through it and to write it.
Cariwalt

Carrie Harper Walton, Author

Phyllis M Olmstead, Editor

Charles Walton Enterprises LLC Cover Concept

You Are Already Healed!!!

Carrie Harper Walton, Author

Phyllis M Olmstead, Editor

Charles Walton Enterprises LLC Cover Concept

Facebook: You Are Already Healed

All scriptures are from the King James Version (KJV) of the Bible.

Olmstead Publishing LLC
www.OlmsteadPublishing.com
www.facebook.com/olmsteadpublishing

Printed in the United States of America
ISBN 978-1-93419425-6 1-934194-25-5

Cari@Minister.Com
www.GAPWarriorsMinistry.Org

Contents

Carrie Harper Walton

Feel free to make notes, underline, or highlight any text
in this book that stirs your spirit.

Dedication

I dedicate this book foremost to my Lord and
Savior Jesus Christ, Yeshua, which is His name in
Hebrew, so it must be His name in the Greek. The
name that is high and above every name; the name
that His people find so sacred they make sure they
do not damage it. The name that I apply to and the
name that I subject each and every petition I send
up to Him to because I know that name works. He
is my Christ; He most definitely is my Lord, and
Savior. However, His true and declared name, and
I revere it, is Yeshua.

I then dedicate this book to my Spiritual Head, my
pastor, my confidante, the one and only daddy of
all my children, the one and only husband I have
ever known, my best friend, sometimes it feels like
my only friend; Eugene Walton, D.D.

I cannot make this dedication without adding my
three daughters to this list: Pamela Jeanean, Faith
Elania, and Hope Victoria. I thank God for them
and I take this and every other opportunity to say
how very proud I am of them. God, whose Hebrew

name is Yahweh, did an awesome job raising my girls and I give Him all the credit He so richly deserves. I add each of their husband's to this list: Anthony, Chris, and Sheldon.

I can never forget my three grandchildren, the joy of me and my husband's hearts; Christopher, Charity and Joshua Eugene (G'anny love you guys so much—I thank God for each of you, as I lift you up in prayer daily. You keep me going and feeling active—you are better for me than taking two shots of vitamin B-12).

I include and dedicate this book to all of my family members that we have prayed for over the years, those for which we are standing in the GAP and on the Word of God. Thank you, because I know we will see the moving of God in you very soon.

I thank all of you for your love and support.   ✞

Author

Pastor Carrie Harper Walton, founder of GAP
Warriors Ministry,
graduated from
Florida State
University in 1975
with a Bachelor of
Arts degree in special
education. Carrie then

attended International Seminary in Orlando, FL in
1979 under Dr. Glen E. Tyler.

Pastor Carrie, as she is fondly called, started her
career by ministering with her husband, Dr.
Eugene Walton, at Fort Myer United States Army
post in Arlington, Virginia. Their congregation
consisted of members from all branches of the
military, government workers, and civilians. The
military congregation's gospel choir conducted an
east coast concert tour in 1982, ministering at
civilian venues and military bases, singing and
sharing the word of God. Pastor Carrie and Dr.
Walton held a bible study class for the troops and
served as adjunct professors for their seminary.

Several of those troops from their tutelage are pastors today.

In 1987, the Walton's ministered for three weeks in Anambra State, Nigeria, West Africa, where around 1,500 souls heard and came to Christ. The couple saw firsthand how and why the work for the Kingdom is so huge in Africa today. The preachers could see the people's childlike faith in God's word even in the 1980's. This trip proved to be a true faith-builder for Pastor Carrie. Many events challenged and tested her faith but she and Dr. Walton continued to trust God and walk in their convictions. Pastor Carrie's faith and belief in God's Power increased dramatically during her time in Africa.

Pastor Carrie has traveled to Brussels' Belgium; Zurich, Switzerland; Cabo San Lucas, Mexico; the Bahamas; Vancouver, Canada; the Caribbean; Rosetta, Mexico; and London, England. Wherever she traveled, God always blessed and she always found someone to talk with and for whom to pray.

Pastor Carrie has served as the CEO of the Medical Emergency Network, President of Maryland Insurance Academy, Executive Vice President on the Walton Group and Diversified Consultants. She was affiliated with Concerned Women for America (a Christian lobbying group on Capitol Hill) and has been listed in a Who's Who in America publication. Pastor Carrie has served as a guest speaker at several women's conferences and various prayer events.

Pastor Carrie met Eugene Walton in 1967 and they married almost 40 years ago. Of the 46 years, they have known each other, 35 of those years she co-pastored and co-authored in the ministry with her husband. They love tag-team teaching in seminars and conferences.

They complement each other, sometimes finishing each other's sentences. One day, when Dr. Walton came back to the car after picking up something from the grocery store Pastor Carrie heard him singing. They were singing not only the same song, but also the very same verse. She firmly believes and frequently says that God put them together.

In 1996, God birthed in Pastor Carrie's spirit *GAP Warriors Ministry* (God's Anointed Prayer Warriors). A ministry where God enables dedicated Prayer Warriors to STAND in the GAP for those who cannot stand firm for themselves at a crucial time in their life. This ministry has seen the hand of God work miracles over these past 16 years and He is still showing He is God all by Himself! Many situations in the GAP Ministry inspired Pastor Carrie to create the *Healing Scriptures* CD in 2007-2008.

Pastor Carrie, prayerfully, will finish her doctorate degree very soon. She and Dr. Walton continue to allow the Spirit of the Lord to use them. The Devil continues to try to stop their work. Dr. Walton has had special battles over the past two years, **but** by their touching and agreeing on God's Word, God has given them the victory again. They are holding more seminars through the *Traveling Fisherman Ministry* as they continue praying and standing in the GAP.

Pastor Carrie and Dr. Walton are always ready and awaiting the call to serve—teaching, preaching, seminars, workshops, etc., always standing with and on the Word of God. ☩

Purpose of the *Healing Scriptures*

This book, *You are Already Healed!!!,* can be considered medicine on paper. In 2007, I, Carrie Harper Walton, recorded this book as a CD. There was no intent to write this book until my husband's diagnosis with stage-four cancer, his kidneys shutting down, and hearing that he had only 6-weeks to live. Up until 2010, I actually gave most of the *Healing Scripture* CDs away to people God led me toward and those that others told me were sick. Looking back, God was using simple cases with me. I did not know that He was testing and training me for the BIGGIES that were to come.

When I made the CD, I was just following the lead of the Holy Spirit. To be honest, I really did not think it would amount to very much. I remember thinking and even discussing that fact, as I saw it. Many other people had already made this type of CD and the concept was not new. I had to laugh at myself because the Lord reminded me that if something is **new** then it probably is **not true** and if it was **true** it definitely is **not new**, for "there is no new thing under the sun" Ecclesiastes 1:9.

Carrie Harper Walton

Further, He let me know that those other CDs were for and by someone else, they were not for the same people. He continued rebuking me by sharing with my spirit that I would be a BOLD witness with my version as those other authors were with theirs. He let me know He was able to multi-task; He had no problem directing more than one person at a time. Even with each person doing more than one task. He finished by impressing the need for me to be quiet and get started. Although, the way God relayed that point to me was much more cordial, warm, and amiable. I knew what He meant.

That very night I started going through the *Holy Bible* searching for all of the healing scriptures. I did not realize how very important they would become in my life; how those same scriptures would come alive to my family and me.

You see, in 2010, I saw my husband's body touched by prostate cancer and I watched my 250-pound husband lose 60 pounds in three weeks.

One night, my husband was in bed and he became very cold, I put five heavy blankets on him, yet I could still see him shaking. I knew the Devil was whispering to him, I have been there and he had done it to me. The Lord told me to get my dear husband's mind focused on the Word. I looked at my husband, a strong man of God that I had known most of my life, fighting not only the pain and sickness in his body but those death thoughts the Devil was trying to sow in his spirit. I put the *Healing Scriptures* in the CD-player, put the headphones on his ears, and told him to repeat each scripture and confession along with the CD. There were 45 scriptures on that CD, and by God's grace, he repeated every one of those scriptures.

The amazing thing was that he was shaking so strongly that no one could understand what he was saying. I sat next to him the entire time, praying and knowing God's Word was healing him. I did not care what I heard and what I saw, I just clung to God's Word. It was during the 32nd scripture of the CD when I began to hear and understand what my husband was saying. It was like the breaking of a fever. I opened my eyes, his body had stopped shaking, he became calm, and his words and praising of God were so very clear.

I knew our break-through had come. I realized then that I had never cried. I still could not, there was still too much to accomplish. "Maybe later," I thought.

On December 7, 2010, Dr. Woods, my husband's urologist, told us he had an aggressive form of cancer and they would operate the next day; it was just that serious. There was no time to think or ponder over anything. However, I have to say, I truly thank God for my husband's doctor. He is a man that is really after God's heart. This man really cares for people, and realizing all answers come from God, he listens to God for how and what to do for his patients.

The next day the doctor said he was going to operate on my husband last instead of at 1:00 pm as scheduled. They were going to do a biopsy so they would not have to wait for the answer. He then said, "Last night God told me what to do to save your husband's life." He told us the procedure and I immediately said, "Then you do what God told you to do."

I put my faith and trust in God and I knew everything would be all right. Dr. Woods did not have to take out my husband's prostate gland and he did not order radiation or chemotherapy treatments. Almost two years later Dr. Walton is cancer free. We give all praise, honor, and glory to God.   ✞

The Inspiration for this Book

Scriptural Foundations for Healing
"Great is thy Faithfulness"

Throughout my life, I remember several medical situations that the doctors felt were very serious. I had rheumatic fever as a child. I awoke one morning and tried to get out of bed. Instead of standing, I fell on the floor in pain that was so great I could only scream. All of my joints, my ankles, knees, and even my elbows felt as though they were broken and piercing into my body.

Another time, during the Thanksgiving holidays, I went into the hospital to have my tonsils removed while I was on the operating table the organ burst. Poison streamed throughout my system. I remained in the hospital until almost Christmas.

In 1975, my father died. He was the one who showed me the type of man to look for in a husband. In 1980, my mother died. She was the one who taught me how to fight for my marriage and work to provide my family a clean, loving, giving, respectful, and wholesome home.

On November 17, 1980, my youngest child was born during the sixth month of my pregnancy because I had developed a staph infection. The doctor said, "I can only save the baby or Mrs. Walton, not both of them." My husband and I prayed God's Word, and put our total trust in Him.

My daughter did survive and she remained in the Neonatal Intensive Care Unit (NICU) at Walter Reed Army Hospital for three months. She remained on the respirator for three months. Her heart stopped beating three times. Her lungs collapsed three times. In addition, she required open-heart surgery at only 30 days old.

Today, Hope Victoria and I are both alive and well. My daughter **gives God the glory** in song and she started her own record label called Child of God Records.

I went with my husband to West Africa for three-weeks during the mid-1980s to conduct a crusade throughout Anambra state, Nigeria. I began hemorrhaging upon our arrival and the bleeding continued the entire time we were there. My husband and I ministered in heat in excess of 110 degrees, but I refused to allow it to stop me. Upon my return to the United States, I immediately admitted myself to a hospital where I had a large cyst removed from my ovary and discovered I had carried my twin in my right ovary for 34 years.

There have been times in my life when I have suffered from pain, various infections, and even the unbelievable stress from the loss of my last daughter, who we named Patience. She died right after she was born, but gave me several hours of joy and love.

There have also been times of great emotional stress and danger. In February 1998, an F-5 tornado destroyed our home and all our family possessions, but God preserved all our lives during this tornado. He even allowed me to see the very center of that funnel, to experience being inside it and to have victory over it.

After the 9/11/2011 terrorist attacks, the stock market crash destroyed my husband's business.

We lost everything except out faith in God. Now, I can understand how the prophet Job of the *Holy Bible* felt. It is during these times, times of great turmoil and loss, that people shun you. They are afraid you are going to ask for something, especially those of which you forgave their debts. Some people said my family was not saved, some declared we must have done something wrong, and some just laughed at us. Those who laughed were actually glad about our circumstances.

Throughout my life, I have learned and taught my girls, that regardless of what was thrown at me or my family that we had to pick up the pieces and go on. There was no time to waste crying or feeling sorry for ourselves. In these times, you have to believe that God knows what He is doing. We just have to continue to love the people and let God handle each situation.

I know God has put doctors here for us. I also thank God that all of the doctors that He placed in my life, I believe they were all gifts from God to me. I believe they were all God-fearing men and women, especially Dr. Woods. Each of these

Carrie Harper Walton

doctors admitted they were limited alone, but complete in and with God. While it is a **fact** that man's knowledge has increased, we need to admit that man is not all knowing. There is a higher Truth—The Word of God.

As you read this book, please do not place a time constraint on your healing. Just stay with it until you achieve victory. God has the time schedule but you have the victory and **God alone gets the glory**. In my life, I have seen some instant miracles but the healings were gradual. Give God time to talk to you about those challenges you are experiencing. Do not be too busy to hear or deal with the situation. Healing is usually gradual so you can have some God time—just you and Him.

Let us address first things first! We must recognize that our healing was already <u>bought and paid for</u> by the **Lord Jesus Christ**. Healing is part of the salvation package that we receive when we are born-again. We do not deny that failure, stress, sickness, and disease are present in our lives however, and we are denying them the right to stay in our lives, especially in our bodies. By receiving the truth of what was purchased for us at Calvary we then know and accept that healing is our gift, our blessing from the Lord!

When you finally come to the place, that state of mind, where you are ready to receive your healing by faith, ☐ **write down** the date and resolve it before the Lord. From that day forward you will no longer **ask** the Lord for healing, instead you will begin to thank Him and praise Him **for** your healing.

This is where the battle begins. In the days to come the enemy will attempt to talk you out of this claim. He will try to convince you it did not work or it is not for you. You must stand strong in faith and not give in. Retreat is **not** an option.

When the enemy says you are not healed, you can now state unequivocally with complete confidence,

"On this date ☐, Devil, I received, I accepted, and I acknowledged my healing. YES, I time-honor the healing that is already mine."

Tell Satan,

"I receive my healing by faith. You are just too late! I know God's Word is His will for me. Hear me well. I take my healing. It is mine! ***I am already healed!!!"*** ✠

Background of God's Healing Scriptures

As we begin to study our *Healing Scriptures*, let us get a clearer understanding of the power found in God's Word.

The Hebrew word for "**medicine**" used in Proverbs 17:22 "*A merry heart doeth good like a medicine: but a broken spirit drieth the bones*" is גֵּהָה—**gēhâ** which means, a cure; a healing (Strong's Concordance, H1456). The *Holy Bible* tells us in Proverbs 4:22 that the Word of God is "*health to all our flesh*". The Hebrew word here for health is "מַרְפֵּא—**marpē'** which means healing, cure, and remedy (Strong's Concordance, H4832). We will learn that the medicine God prescribes is His Word.

Many people make the mistake of substituting belief in healing for the actual taking of God's medicine; His medicine is His Word.
Many will say they believe in healing but they have never actually taken the medicine, they have never really heard nor believed in His Word. As

we study the Word of God, we do as David said; hide His Word and His Commandments in our hearts. Just think, what good would it be for you to believe in food if you did not eat it? If you did not eat the food, you would starve. The same is true for medicine; it would do you no good if you did not take it. Well, God's Word is medicine to our flesh.

Let us take a moment and look at several parallels between God's medicine and natural medicine. First, as we look at God's Word, we see that God's Word is a healing agent, just the same as prescribed medicine is to our body. The Word of God is no respecter of persons, just as prescribed medicine has the same uniqueness; it will work for anyone who takes it. In addition, when we think about it, all medicine must be taken according to directions to be effective.

Some medicine labels state, "take internally". Other labels say, "use externally". If you put the medicine on your body externally when the direction say to take it internally, the medicine may not work. Taking it after a meal, when directions say take it before the meal, will reduce its effectiveness. Taking it occasionally, when the directions say to take it three times a day, will limit the results. No matter how good the medicine is, it must be taken according to the directions or it will not work.

Therefore, God's medicine must be taken according to directions for it to work. God's Word must get into the midst of your heart and stay there in order to heal your body. Head knowledge is not sufficient. God's Words must penetrate your spirit-man through meditation. Solomon said, meditating both day and night–attending, hearing, looking, pondering–to produce healing in your body. Once the Word penetrates you, it will bring health to all of your flesh.

Remember, for your medicine to work You must take it. Start Declaring the Word and Confess your healing—YOU ARE ALREADY HEALED—in Jesus' name.   ☩

Reading of the *Healing Scriptures*

> **DIRECTIONS:** This medicine must be taken 2 to 3 times a day depending upon the need and condition of the patient.

The following scriptures are excerpts from the *Healing Scriptures* CD I completed in 2008. As you read this book, please pay close attention and intently take note. Adhere to what the Word of God says about who you are in Christ. You must realize that healing takes place not based upon your feelings, but your faith in God's Word.

You will see yourself having a paradigm shift from how you used to perceive things. Your faith will grow and your situation will begin to change as you put into action that which you believe and know. You must feed your faith and starve your doubts to death. God's Word is medicine to all our flesh. The Lord is our physician and the medicine that He prescribes is His precious Word.

God's Word is a healing agent. It has the capacity to produce healing within our bodies. God sent His

Word and it healed. His Word is alive and full of positive energy. *The Word of God is the life of God.* The *Holy Bible* tells us to listen to God's Words and do not ignore them. They produce healing in your body and they bring health to all your flesh, Proverb 4:22, "For they *are* life unto those that find them, and health to all their flesh."

In my seeking the Lord concerning healing, He so graciously revealed to me what I was doing wrong, those things I was missing concerning my healing. Walking me through His Word, He armed me with the tools I needed so I could take hold of what He had promised us through His redemptive plan. I have experienced healing within my body. With this book, I shall walk you through those same healing scriptures, sharing the truth, declarations, and confessions that the Holy Spirit showed me. The key to partaking of the life and healing energy in the Word is feeding on it until it penetrates your spirit where it deposits that life and energy.

When Peter said in Acts 10:34b, "God is no respector of persons" and in Romans 2:11, "For there is no respect of persons with God," he meant

Carrie Harper Walton

that God does not show favoritism. What He has done for others He will do for you, also. You must feed daily on these scriptures. In fact, you should taste of them several times a day. Regularly repeat these scriptures to yourself to embed them into your spirit.

I promise you the Word of God will work but you must get the Word inside, in your spirit man. You must also start today to declare and confess your healing; you must say it aloud. Jesus spoke the Word to the Devil, "Get thee behind me, Satan." remember the world was spoken into being and it became alive (Luke 4:8, Mark 8:33, Matthew 16:23). We must speak the Word to the Devil, not think it, but **speak** it so it will come alive. Every time you declare a scripture, you are submitting yourself for healing. Learn to speak health to your body, subjecting and calling out that illness to Yeshua. Remember, "Death and life are in the power of the tongue. (Proverbs 18:21a)"

Many Christians say, "The shortest distance between a problem and a solution is the distance between your knees and the ground." In addition,

"The one who kneels and prays before the Lord can stand up to anything." As we pray, we should always expect a miracle.   ✟

Let's Go!

Now proceed on to the listing of *Healing Scriptures*—which is your inheritance! Meditate on them; focus on them. Begin to see yourself in the light of the promises of God. See yourself as the Word says you are! The Lord paid an extremely high price for you to enjoy the benefit of all of His promises. Do not speak your problem, but begin to speak the answer, God's Word, and watch your situations and conditions begin to change!!! As you read each CONFESSION, make it personal, from **you to God**. ✞

Let Us Pray

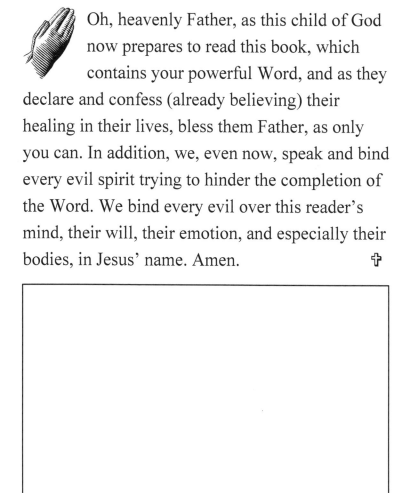

Oh, heavenly Father, as this child of God now prepares to read this book, which contains your powerful Word, and as they declare and confess (already believing) their healing in their lives, bless them Father, as only you can. In addition, we, even now, speak and bind every evil spirit trying to hinder the completion of the Word. We bind every evil over this reader's mind, their will, their emotion, and especially their bodies, in Jesus' name. Amen.   ✞

Genesis

📖 THE BIBLE DECLARES

Gen 1:28   And God blessed them, and God said unto them, be fruitful, and multiply, and replenish the earth, and subdue it; and have dominion over the fish of the sea, and over the fowl of the air, and over every living thing that moveth upon the earth. (KJV)

I CONFESS ⸲

Lord, I know for a fact that when my body is in an alkaline state some illnesses, like cancer, cannot thrive. The same is required of the Word of God, for it requires the blood cells in my body also to obey as they develop and refill daily within my body.

Lord, Your Word gives me power and authority over every living thing and that includes cancer, bacteria, parasites, viruses, and all microorganisms that cause sickness and diseases to attack my body. Furthermore, Father, Your greatest gift was Your Word. I put my foot down on sickness and disease and command, not ask, but command, they leave my body right now. You know my blood was purchased by the shed **blood** of Jesus Christ. Lord, thank You for releasing me and giving me dominion over sickness in my body. I speak life not death, and healing and health throughout my body and I ask it in the powerful name of Jesus. I know that it is done. Thank you, Lord!

THE BIBLE DECLARES

Gen 6:3 "And the LORD said, 'My spirit shall not always strive with man, for that he also is flesh: yet his days shall be an hundred and twenty years.'" (KJV)

I CONFESS

Lord, Your Word said You have provided me the right to a long life, no more than 120 years, if I so desire.

I speak to every illness even death, you will not over take me. Satan, you will not overshadow my thoughts, and I command you to release my mind, will, emotion, and my body.

Father, I stand on your promise for long life. I will not give in to anything.

Devil, I refuse to let you steal anything else from me ever again. I have work and I am going to live. Hear me, Satan! I am going to live! I am going to live and not die.

Lord, I speak life not death, and healing and health throughout my body and I ask it in the powerful name of Jesus! I know that it is done. Thank you, Lord! ✝

Exodus

📖 THE BIBLE DECLARES

Exodus 15:26 "And said, If thou wilt diligently hearken to the voice of the LORD thy God, and wilt do that which is right in his sight, and wilt give ear to his commandments, and keep all his statutes, I will put none of these diseases upon thee, which I have brought upon the Egyptians: for I am the LORD that healeth thee." (KJV)

I CONFESS ₹

Lord, I thank you for this word. Lord I know you are speaking directly to me. I know healing is taking place in my body right now. Lord, Your Word is more than able to heal me. I know your Word is full of healing power. I speak healing right now! You are my Savior and I thank you for coming into my life. Lord, heal me of all illness and attacks by the Devil. When sickness tries to touch my body, I bind it in Jesus' name. Lord, I take comfort in knowing You have never left me. Lord, I know my body will respond to Your command, Your Word that I am healed. Lord, I know healing is in God and the Spirit of God is in me. I am healed! Lord, I speak life not death, and healing and health throughout my body and I ask it in the powerful name of Jesus. I know that it is done! Thank You, Lord!

📖 THE BIBLE DECLARES

Exodus 23:25 "And ye shall serve the LORD your God, and he shall bless thy bread, and thy water; and I will take sickness away from the midst of thee."

I CONFESS ⸴

Lord, with all my heart, soul, and mind I know that You are real and Your Word is also real. I know right now, Lord, You are speaking to this sickness; letting sickness know he must let go and cannot linger when the Lord's Spirit is in me.

Sickness, you must go. I speak to you, Sickness, and I bind every evil present in my body. I bind even the evil in the atmosphere.

Lord, I speak life not death, and healing and health throughout my body and I ask it in the powerful name of Jesus. I know that it is done! Thank You, Lord! ✞

Leviticus

📖 THE BIBLE DECLARES

Leviticus 18:4-5 "Ye shall do my judgments, and keep mine ordinances, to walk therein: I am the LORD your God. Ye shall therefore keep my statutes, and my judgments: which if a man does, he shall live in them: I am the LORD." (KJV)

I CONFESS ⸮

Every day, Lord, I am seeking to get closer to You. I want Your Word in my heart, Lord. Revive me daily, Lord, from the trials of this world. I am not sick. I am not discouraged. I am prosperous and healed. Lord, I speak life not death, and healing and health throughout my body and I ask it in the powerful name of Jesus! I know that it is done. Thank you, Lord! ✞

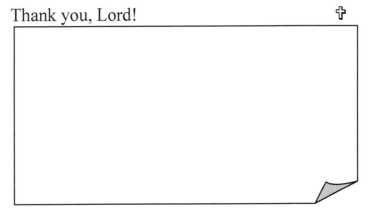

Deuteronomy

📖 THE BIBLE DECLARES
Deut 7:15 "And the LORD will take away from thee all sickness, and will put none of the evil diseases of Egypt, which thou knowest, upon thee; but will lay them upon all them that hate thee". (KJV)

I CONFESS ⸠
Thank You. Thank You. I thank You, Lord for making Your Word so simple and so clear. I know that both healing and good health belong to me, thank You, Lord. Your Word has revealed to me my rights, my legacy, and I refuse to let go of my blessing from You, Lord. I am healed. Lord, I speak life not death, and healing and health throughout my body and I ask it in the powerful name of Jesus! I know that it is done. Thank you, Lord!

📖 THE BIBLE DECLARES
Deut. 29:29 "The secret things belong unto the LORD our God: but those things which are

revealed belong unto us and to our children for ever, that we may do all the words of this law."

I CONFESS ⦃

The Word is true and so clear that my healing and health belong to my family and me. I dig in and take hold of it by faith and I refuse to let go of my birthright, Lord. I speak life not death, and healing and health throughout my body and I ask it in the powerful name of Jesus. I know that it is done. Thank You, Lord!

📖 THE BIBLE DECLARES

Deut 30:19-20 "I call heaven and earth to record this day against you, that I have set before you life and death, blessing and cursing: therefore choose life, that both thou and thy seed may live: That thou mayest love the LORD thy God, and that thou mayest obey his voice, and that thou mayest cleave unto him: for he is thy life, and the length of thy days: that thou mayest dwell in the land which the LORD sware unto thy fathers, to Abraham, to Isaac, and to Jacob, to give them."

I CONFESS ⸢

I thank You, Lord, for I choose life. You made that choice possible for me. I know that with Your Word in my heart, You will not fail me for I have been added to Your family and I have fallen in love with You and Your Word. Lord, I speak life not death, and healing and health throughout my body and I ask it in the powerful name of Jesus! I know that it is done. Thank you, Lord! ☧

Joshua

📖 THE BIBLE DECLARES

Joshua 21:45 "There failed not ought of any good thing which the LORD had spoken unto the house of Israel; all came to pass." (KJV)

I CONFESS ⅔

Lord, You died for me and I hold to Your promises in my heart. Your Word is true and I thank You for the blood You shed for I know that I am healed. Your Word assures me of this. Lord, I speak life not death, and healing and health throughout my body and I ask it in the powerful name of Jesus! I know that it is done. Thank You, Lord! ✟

Job

📖 THE BIBLE DECLARES

Job 22:26-28 "For then shalt thou have thy delight in the Almighty, and shalt lift up thy face unto God. Thou shalt make thy prayer unto him, and he shall hear thee, and thou shalt pay thy vows. Thou shalt also decree a thing, and it shall be established unto thee: and the light shall shine upon thy ways." (KJV)

I CONFESS ⸱

Lord, I speak all Your promises in your Word. They are my inheritance. I know that I am healed. Lord, You paid the price for my healing. Then You allowed them to beat You. Because of You, Lord, I can speak Your Word and tell Satan, "I am healed." Life not death, and healing and health throughout my body and I ask it in the powerful name of Jesus. I know that it is done. Thank You, Lord! ✝

Psalm

📖 THE BIBLE DECLARES
Ps 30:2 "O LORD my God, I cried unto thee, and thou hast healed me." (KJV)

I CONFESS ⧼
With all my heart, soul, and mind, Lord, I am healed. You have healed me. I don't care how I feel and I look not at my circumstances, but with all my heart I believe I am healed. Lord, You have healed me. Life not death, and healing and health throughout my body and I ask it in the powerful name of Jesus. I know that it is done. Thank You, Lord!

📖 THE BIBLE DECLARES
Ps. 34:19 "Many are the afflictions of the righteous: but the LORD delivereth him out of them all."

I CONFESS ⧼
Lord, I know with all my heart I am already healed. Lord, I know You delivered me from the hands of Satan. I love You, Lord. Lord, I speak life

not death, and healing and health throughout my body and I ask it in the powerful name of Jesus. I know that it is done! Thank You, Lord!

📖 THE BIBLE DECLARES

Ps. 41:3 "The LORD will strengthen him upon the bed of languishing: thou wilt make all his bed in his sickness."

I CONFESS ⋸

Thank You, Lord, for healing every condition trying to touch my body. I know, Lord, You will turn my afflictions into dances. Lord, I speak life not death, and healing and health throughout my body and I ask it in the powerful name of Jesus. I know that it is done. Thank You, Lord!

📖 THE BIBLE DECLARES

Ps. 42:11 "Why art thou cast down, O my soul? And why art thou disquieted within me? Hope thou in God: for I shall yet praise him, who is the health of my countenance, and my God."

I CONFESS ᚐ

Lord, I am not discouraged for I will overcome any challenge. I do not doubt Your Word, Lord. I remain unwavering and unmovable. Lord, I speak life not death, and healing and health throughout my body and I ask it in the powerful name of Jesus. I know that it is done. Thank You, Lord!

THE BIBLE DECLARES

Ps. 91:1-10 "He that dwelleth in the secret place of the most high shall abide under the shadow of the Almighty. I will say of the LORD, He is my refuge and my fortress: my God; in him will I trust. Surely he shall deliver thee from the snare of the fowler, and from the noisome pestilence. He shall cover thee with his feathers, and under his wings shalt thou trust: his truth shall be thy shield and buckler. Thou shalt not be afraid for the terror by night; nor for the arrow that flieth by day; Nor for the pestilence that walketh in darkness; nor for the destruction that wasteth at noonday. A thousand shall fall at thy side, and ten thousand at thy right hand; but it shall not come nigh thee. Only with thine eyes shalt thou behold and see the reward of the wicked. Because thou hast made the LORD, which is my refuge, even the most High, thy habitation; there shall no evil befall thee, neither shall any plague come nigh thy dwelling."

I CONFESS ≷

Lord, I know it is You that heals me. I know I can hide within You and You will shelter me from all sickness and disease. I thank You, Lord, for the protection of Your Word against all sickness. I know that even Your wings have healing in them. I speak life not death, and healing and health throughout my body and I ask it in the powerful name of Jesus. I know that it is done. Thank You, Lord!

📖 THE BIBLE DECLARES

Ps. 91:16 "With long life will I satisfy him, and shew him my salvation."

I CONFESS ≷

I thank You, Lord, for Your Word, for in You I have no wants or needs. Lord, I speak life not death, and healing and health throughout my body and I ask it in the powerful name of Jesus. I know that it is done. Thank You, Lord!

📖 THE BIBLE DECLARES

Ps. 102:19-20 "For he hath looked down from the height of his sanctuary; from heaven did the LORD behold the earth; to hear the groaning of the prisoner; to loose those that are appointed to death;"

I CONFESS ≷

Lord, thank You for setting me free. I hold to my covenant right (those promises from God) and I command Satan, sickness, disease, pain, and suffering to get out of my life and leave me alone. Lord, I speak life not death, and healing and health throughout my body and I ask it in the powerful name of Jesus. I know that it is done. Thank You, Lord!

📖 THE BIBLE DECLARES

Ps. 103:2-3 "Bless the LORD, O my soul, and forget not all his benefits: Who forgiveth all thine iniquities; who healeth all thy diseases;"

I CONFESS ⧼

I bless You, Lord. I praise You and I thank You for all You have given to me. You forgave my sins, my faults, my failures, and my disobedience. You healed all my diseases and I love You. I speak life not death, and healing and health throughout my body and I ask it in the powerful name of Jesus. I know that it is done. Thank You, Lord!

📖 THE BIBLE DECLARES

Ps. 107:20 "He sent his word, and healed them, and delivered them from their destructions."

I CONFESS ⧼

Thank You, Father, for giving me Your precious Word; it has delivered me. I know Your Word is more than able to do what it says. I know Your Word is healing me right now. I know there is power in Your Word. Lord, I speak life not death, and healing and health throughout my body and I ask it in the powerful name of Jesus. I know that it is done. Thank You, Lord!

Carrie Harper Walton

📖 THE BIBLE DECLARES

Ps. 118:17 "I shall not die, but live, and declare the works of the LORD."

I CONFESS ⦃

Lord, I stand in agreement with Your Word. I know you have a road map for me and I refuse to let Satan take my blessings from me. Lord, I speak life not death, and healing and health throughout my body and I ask it in the powerful name of Jesus. I know that it is done. Thank You, Lord!

📖 THE BIBLE DECLARES

Ps. 119:50 "This is my comfort in my affliction: for thy word hath quickened me."

I CONFESS ⦃

Lord, according to Your Word, I claim health to all my flesh. Your Word is my remedy against Satan's fiery darts charging after me daily. Lord, I speak life not death, and healing and health throughout my body and I ask it in the powerful name of Jesus. I know that it is done. Thank You, Lord! ✝

Proverbs

📖 THE BIBLE DECLARES

Prov. 3:7-8 "Be not wise in thine own eyes: fear the LORD, and depart from evil. [8] It shall be health to thy navel, and marrow to thy bones." (KJV)

I CONFESS ⸱

I worship You in all things, Lord. I cannot depend upon my own understanding, but I trust You for You have never failed me. I trust You only, Lord. Lord, I speak life not death, and healing and health throughout my body and I ask it in the powerful name of Jesus. I know that it is done. Thank You, Lord!

📖 THE BIBLE DECLARES

Prov. 4:20-22 "My son, attend to my words; incline thine ear unto my sayings. Let them not depart from thine eyes; keep them in the midst of thine heart. For they are life unto those that find them, and health to all their flesh."

I CONFESS ⌇

Your Word, Lord, is true and powerful. Your Word energizes me and it is full of life. Your healing power is found in Your Word. That same healing power is at work in me **right now**. I feel it cleaning every area of my body. The healing virtue is detoxing my body, pulling out all of spiritual toxins from me.

Come out, Impurities, and come in Cleansing agents.

Lord, I speak life not death, and healing and health throughout my body and I ask it in the powerful name of Jesus. I know that it is done. Thank You, Lord!

📖 THE BIBLE DECLARES

Prov. 12:18 "There is that speaketh like the piercings of a sword: but the tongue of the wise is health." (KJV)

I CONFESS ⌇

Lord, I know I can speak sickness or health into my body and I choose health. I know that I must say, "I am healed." for **I AM THAT I AM** (the Creator that spoke the world into existence) has healed me. **I AM THAT I AM** is a body regulator (εἰμί— **eimi**, Strong's Concordance, G1510; Ex 3:14). I speak only the positive in my life for when I see the ✝ cross, I see only + positive. Lord, I speak life not death, and healing and health throughout my body and I ask it in the powerful name of Jesus. I know that it is done. Thank You, Lord!

📖 THE BIBLE DECLARES
Prov. 17:22 "A merry heart doeth good like a medicine: but a broken spirit drieth the bones".

I CONFESS ⸔
Lord, I believe in Your Word and I know Your Word is powerful. Your Word gives me a merry heart. If I feel sick, down, depressed and I begin to dwell on Your Word I become stronger in my mind and in my body. When discouraged I read Your Word and it brings joy and a smile to my face and my heart. When I speak the Word it touches my spirit and transforms my cells from the attacks of sickness into a strong working machine able to fight a little longer. Thank You for Your

Carrie Harper Walton

Word. Lord, I speak life not death, and healing and health throughout my body and I ask it in the powerful name of Jesus. I know that it is done. Thank You, Lord!   ☦

Isaiah

📖 THE BIBLE DECLARES

Isa. 33:24 "And the inhabitant shall not say, I am sick: the people that dwell therein shall be forgiven their iniquity." (KJV)

I CONFESS ⸱

Thank You, Lord, for the forgiveness of my sins. Oh, Lord, Your forgiveness makes me happy to forgive others. That forgiveness helps heal my body faster. Thank You, Lord.

I forgive you, _____, I forgive you ,_____, I forgive you, _____, and you, _____.

Lord, I am healing. Lord, I speak Life not death, and healing and health throughout my body and I ask it in the powerful name of Jesus. I know that it is done. Thank You, Lord!

📖 THE BIBLE DECLARES

Isa. 40:31 "But they that wait upon the LORD shall renew their strength; they shall mount up with wings as eagles; they shall run, and not be weary; and they shall walk, and not faint."

I CONFESS ⋜

Lord, I do not care how the Devil comes against me and, at times, how he is touching every area of my life, body, spirit, and soul. Lord, I know if I continue to stand on Your Word, You will preserve me through all I must endure. Lord, I do not pray my trials and tribulations away; I ask that you give me the strength to get through them. I know they make me stronger. Lord, I speak life not death, and healing and health throughout my body and I ask it in the powerful name of Jesus. I know that it is done. Thank You, Lord!

📖 THE BIBLE DECLARES

Isa. 43:25-26 "I, even I, am he that blotteth out thy transgressions for mine own sake, and will not remember thy sins. Put me in remembrance: let us plead together: declare thou, that thou mayest be justified."

I CONFESS ⁒

Lord, I claim my total healing. The debt for my
healing was paid in full on the ✟ cross over 2,000
years ago. I thank and praise You, for You are my
Lord and Savior. I speak life not death, and healing
and health throughout my body and I ask it in the
powerful name of Jesus. I know that it is done.
Thank You, Lord!

📖 THE BIBLE DECLARES

Isa. 53:4-5 "Surely he hath borne our griefs, and
carried our sorrows: yet we did esteem him
stricken, smitten of God, and afflicted. But he was
wounded for our transgressions; he was bruised for
our iniquities: the chastisement of our peace was
upon him; and with his stripes we are healed."

I CONFESS ⁒

Father, the scriptures assure me that Your Word is
true and accurate and I believe. I thank you for
being wounded [hurt and injured] for me. Thank
You, Lord, for taking my transgressions [sins]. I
want to thank You, Father, for being bruised
[beaten] for me. You then took the chastisement
[punishment I deserved] upon yourself, [so I would not

have to take it; so I could find peace] and because of you doing all of this, I have healing in my life. Lord, You did not have to do this, but You did it for me. Lord, I speak life not death, and healing and health throughout my body and I ask it in the powerful name of Jesus. I know that it is done. Thank You, Lord!

📖 THE BIBLE DECLARES

Isa. 54:17 "No weapon that is formed against thee shall prosper; and every tongue that shall rise against thee in judgment thou shalt condemn. This is the heritage of the servants of the LORD, and their righteousness is of me, saith the LORD. "

I CONFESS ⸗

Go ahead, Devil, build those weapons of mass sickness and death (WMSD), then watch me pull them down with the power of my tongue! I say, "I am not sick. Sickness and Disease, you have no power over me. Devil, I bind every sickness and disease that you are trying to send after my body for you have no power in my life."

I am already healed. Lord, I speak life not death, and healing and health throughout my body and I ask it in the powerful name of Jesus. I know that it is done. Thank You, Lord!

📖 THE BIBLE DECLARES

Isa. 55:11 "So shall my word be that goeth forth out of my mouth: it shall not return unto me void, but it shall accomplish that which I please, and it shall prosper in the thing whereto I sent it."

I CONFESS ⸮

Lord, I see in Your Word I can stand on my healing simply because You said I can. I know Your Word can do all that it says and more. Lord, I speak life not death, and healing and health throughout my body and I ask it in the powerful name of Jesus. I know that it is done. Thank You, Lord!

📖 THE BIBLE DECLARES

Isa. 57:19 "That if two of you shall agree on earth as touching anything that they shall ask, it shall be done for them of my Father which is in heaven."

Carrie Harper Walton

I CONFESS ⌇

Lord, I speak Your Word and I speak healing. I know You will complete Your Word in my life. I trust you, Lord, and I love trusting Your Word. Lord, I speak life not death, and healing and health throughout my body and I ask it in the powerful name of Jesus. I know that it is done. Thank You, Lord!

📖 THE BIBLE DECLARES

Isa. 58:8 "Then shall thy light break forth as the morning, and thine health shall spring forth speedily: and thy righteousness shall go before thee; the glory of the LORD shall be thy reward."

I CONFESS ⌇

I thank You for restoring my health. Lord, thank You for being my booster that keeps me going through those storms until there is clearing in the weather. I can see clear skies ahead. I thank you, Lord, for my speedy recovery. Lord, I speak life not death, and healing and health throughout my body and I ask it in the powerful name of Jesus. I know that it is done. Thank You, Lord! ✝

Jeremiah

📖 THE BIBLE DECLARES

Jer. 1:12 "Then said the LORD unto me, Thou hast well seen: for I will hasten my word to perform it." (KJV)

I CONFESS ⟨

Lord, I thank You for Your Word and how You bring all things to pass in my life. Lord, I receive Your Word and blessing. I receive my healing. I speak life not death, and healing and health throughout my body and I ask it in the powerful name of Jesus. I know that it is done. Thank You, Lord!

📖 THE BIBLE DECLARES

Jer. 17:14 "Heal me, O LORD, and I shall be healed; save me, and I shall be saved: for thou art my praise."

I CONFESS ⟨

Lord, I claim all my healing. Healing is mine, it is mine **right now**. I have been delivered from the hands of sickness and disease. Lord, I speak life

Carrie Harper Walton

not death, and healing and health throughout my body and I ask it in the powerful name of Jesus. I know that it is done. Thank You, Lord!

📖 THE BIBLE DECLARES

Jer. 23:29 "Is not my word like as a fire? Saith the LORD; and like a hammer that breaketh the rock in pieces?"

I CONFESS 🔊

Lord, with Your Word deep within my spirit, like a crushing force, I know I can fight the toughest and most stubborn challenges in my life. I can do this because of Your Word. I have within me the fuel needed to go on. I know, this fuel will never give out for it keeps me going and forever-safe, Lord. I speak life not death, and healing and health throughout my body and I ask it in the powerful name of Jesus. I know that it is done. Thank You, Lord!

📖 THE BIBLE DECLARES

Jer. 30:17 "For I will restore health unto thee, and I will heal thee of thy wounds, saith the LORD;

because they called thee an Outcast, saying, This is Zion, whom no man seeketh after."

I CONFESS ⚡

Lord, thank You for all Your promises in Your Word. I thank You, Lord, for as I search your Word each day I find more and more promises for me to stand on. My faith keeps renewing and I know that I am healed already. Lord, I speak life not death, and healing and health throughout my body and I ask it in the powerful name of Jesus. I know that it is done. Thank You, Lord!

Jer. 33:6 "Behold, I will bring it health and cure, and I will cure them, and will reveal unto them the abundance of peace and truth."

I CONFESS ⚡

Lord, according to Your Word I have good health. I am free of all disease. I am not only walking, but I am running in good health, Lord. Thank You for my good health. Lord, I speak life not death, and healing and health throughout my body and I ask it in the powerful name of Jesus. I know that it is done. Thank You, Lord! ✝

Nahum

📖 THE BIBLE DECLARES

Nah. 1:7-9 "The LORD is good, a strong hold in the day of trouble; and he knoweth them that trust in him. But with an overrunning flood he will make an utter end of the place thereof, and darkness shall pursue his enemies. What do ye imagine against the LORD? he will make an utter end: affliction shall not rise up the second time." (KJV)

I CONFESS ⦚

As I watch and feel my healing occur, my faith has increased. Thank You, Lord, for renewing my faith and showing me how it grows daily. I speak life not death, and healing and health throughout my body and I ask it in the powerful name of Jesus. I know that it is done. Thank You, Lord! ✝

Malachi

📖 THE BIBLE DECLARES

Mal. 4:2-3 "But unto you that fear my name shall the Sun of righteousness arise with healing in his wings; and ye shall go forth, and grow up as calves of the stall. And ye shall tread down the wicked; for they shall be ashes under the soles of your feet in the day that I shall do this, saith the LORD of hosts." (KJV)

I CONFESS ⸗

I thank You, Lord, for Your healing virtue and I go forth in Your name knowing nothing can overtake me. I walk in assurance of Your healing. I speak life not death, and healing and health throughout my body and I ask it in the powerful name of Jesus. I know that it is done. Thank You, Lord! ✟

Carrie Harper Walton

Matthew

📖 THE BIBLE DECLARES

Matt 8:1-3 "When he was come down from the mountain, great multitudes followed him. And, behold, there came a leper and worshipped him, saying, Lord, if thou wilt, thou canst make me clean. And Jesus put forth his hand, and touched him, saying, I will; be thou clean. And immediately his leprosy was cleansed." (KJV)

I CONFESS ⟨

I thank You, Lord, because You never change and You are always the same. Even when You seem to change or people give new interpretations of Your Word, I know you are the same. That is the comfort You provide. Your Word **never** changes for me or anyone else. If anyone misapplies Your Word, it is not of You. If something is **new** then it is not **true** and if it is **true** it is not **new**. I thank You for healing all disease and sickness. Lord, I speak Life not death, and healing and health throughout my body and I ask it in the powerful name of Jesus. I know that it is done. Thank You, Lord!

📖 THE BIBLE DECLARES

Matt. 8:16-17 "When the evening was come, they brought unto him many that were possessed with devils: and he cast out the spirits with his word, and healed all that were sick: That it might be fulfilled which was spoken by Esaias the prophet, saying, Himself took our infirmities, and bare our sicknesses."

I CONFESS ⸱

I thank You, Lord, for your Word is so powerful and it destroys all sickness. Healing is mine. Thank You, Jesus. You took away all my sin and sickness for I realize, sin is a sickness. Lord, I speak life not death, and healing and health throughout my body and I ask it in the powerful name of Jesus. I know that it is done. Thank You, Lord!

📖 THE BIBLE DECLARES

Matt. 18:18 "Verily I say unto you, Whatsoever ye shall bind on earth shall be bound in heaven: and whatsoever ye shall loose on earth shall be loosed in heaven."

I CONFESS ⦃

Lord, I take the authority You gave to me and I put a stop to sickness in my life. Sickness and pain are not mine. I do not want them. I do not even like them. They will not infect my body. I forbid sickness from even entering my body.

Sickness, you have no right to be here so get out. **I am already healed.**

Lord, I speak life not death, and healing and health throughout my body and I ask it in the powerful name of Jesus. I know that it is done. Thank You, Lord!

📖 THE BIBLE DECLARES

Matt. 18:19 "Again I say unto you, That if two of you shall agree on earth as touching anything that they shall ask, it shall be done for them of my Father which is in heaven"

I CONFESS ⦃

Lord, I must ask for everthing in Your name, believing and it shall be done for Your Word declares it. I am healed in Your name. Lord, I speak life not death, and healing and health throughout my body and I ask it in the powerful name of Jesus. I know that it is done. Thank You, Lord!

THE BIBLE DECLARES

Matt. 21:21 "Jesus answered and said unto them, Verily I say unto you, If ye have faith, and doubt not, ye shall not only do this which is done to the fig tree, but also if ye shall say unto this mountain, Be thou removed, and be thou cast into the sea; it shall be done."

I CONFESS

Lord, I have faith in your Word. I speak it and I am healed. I speak life not death, and healing and health throughout my body and I ask it in the powerful name of Jesus. I know that it is done. Thank You, Lord!   ✝

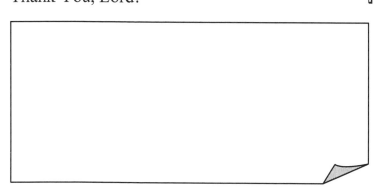

Carrie Harper Walton

Mark

📖 THE BIBLE DECLARES

Mark 5:22-24 "And, behold, there cometh one of the rulers of the synagogue, Jairus by name; and when he saw him, he fell at his feet, And besought him greatly, saying, My little daughter lieth at the point of death: I pray thee, come and lay thy hands on her, that she may be healed; and she shall live. And Jesus went with him; and much people followed him, and thronged him." (KJV)

I CONFESS 🗣

I know there is power in the name Jesus. Thank you, Lord, for You have given me authority over illness. In Your name and in Your Word, I bind sickness and disease in my body right now. I speak life not death, and healing and health throughout my body and I ask it in the powerful name of Jesus. I know that it is done. Thank You, Lord!

📖 THE BIBLE DECLARES

Mark 5:25-34 "And had suffered many things of many physicians, and had spent all that she had, and was nothing bettered, but rather grew worse,

When she had heard of Jesus, came in the press behind, and touched his garment. For she said, If I may touch but his clothes, I shall be whole. And straightway the fountain of her blood was dried up; and she felt in her body that she was healed of that plague. And Jesus, immediately knowing in himself that virtue had gone out of him, turned him about in the press, and said Who touched my clothes? And his disciples said unto him, Thou seest the multitude thronging thee, and sayest thou, Who touched me? And he looked round about to see her that had done this thing. But the woman fearing and trembling, knowing what was done in her, came and fell down before him, and told him all the truth. And he said unto her, Daughter, thy faith hath made thee whole; go in peace, and be whole of thy plague."

I CONFESS ⸱
I thank You, Lord, for my faith in Your Word. Your Word has made me whole. I receive Your power, Lord, for it works in me. My faith allows Your power to do awesome things. I yield myself to you, Lord. I speak life not death, and healing and health throughout my body and I ask it in the

Carrie Harper Walton

powerful name of Jesus. I know that it is done. Thank You, Lord!

📖 THE BIBLE DECLARES

Mark 11:22-23 "And Jesus answering saith unto them, Have faith in God. For verily I say unto you, That whosoever shall say unto this mountain, Be thou removed, and be thou cast into the sea; and shall not doubt in his heart, but shall believe that those things which he saith shall come to pass; he shall have whatsoever he saith."

I CONFESS ≶

I evict sickness and disease from my body. I command, I do not ask, I command sickness and disease to get out of me! I speak to my body, "You are already healed." Lord, I speak life not death, and healing and health throughout my body and I ask it in the powerful name of Jesus. I know that it is done. Thank You, Lord!

📖 THE BIBLE DECLARES

Mark 11:24 "Therefore I say unto you, What things soever ye desire, when ye pray, believe that ye receive them, and ye shall have them."

I CONFESS ⛨

Lord, when I speak according to Your Word. I know I receive what I say. Lord, I speak life not death, and healing and health throughout my body and I ask it in the powerful name of Jesus. I know that it is done. Thank You, Lord!

📖 THE BIBLE DECLARES

Mark 16:17-18 "And these signs shall follow them that believe; In my name shall they cast out devils; they shall speak with new tongues; They shall take up serpents; and if they drink any deadly thing, it shall not hurt them; they shall lay hands on the sick, and they shall recover."

I CONFESS ⛨

I know I receive my healing. I speak recovery to every cell in my body. Lord, I speak Life not death, and healing and health throughout my body and I ask it in the powerful name of Jesus. I know that it is done. Thank You, Lord!   ✝

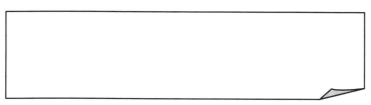

Carrie Harper Walton

Luke

📖 THE BIBLE DECLARES

Luke 10:19 "Behold, I give unto you power to tread on serpents and scorpions, and over all the power of the enemy: and nothing shall by any means hurt you." (KJV)

I CONFESS ⸾

Devil, you have no power over me. Satan, you will get out of my life and take your filthy hands off my body for I am sick and tired of being sick. No more, I bind sickness and I release the Lord's healing virtue throughout my body. I am not scared of you, Devil.

I thank You, Lord, for the authority You gave me. Lord, I speak life not death, and healing and health throughout my body and I ask it in the powerful name of Jesus. I know that it is done. Thank You, Lord!

📖 THE BIBLE DECLARES

Luke 13:11-13 "And, behold, there was a woman which had a spirit of infirmity eighteen years, and was bowed together, and could in no wise lift up herself. And when Jesus saw her, he called her to him, and said unto her, Woman, thou art loosed from thine infirmity. And he laid his hands on her: and immediately she was made straight, and glorified God."

I CONFESS ⸘

Lord, I thank You for my power over the Devil. Your Word has delivered me from Satan's trap.

Sickness, you cannot hold me down. I know Satan is already defeated and when I submit myself to the Spirit and resist him, he must get out of here. He cannot stay or hang around. Healing belongs to me, so take your filthy hands off, Satan.

Lord, I speak life not death, and healing and health throughout my body and I ask it in the powerful name of Jesus. I know that it is done. Thank You, Lord! ☦

Carrie Harper Walton

John

📖 THE BIBLE DECLARES
John 8:36 "If the Son therefore shall make you free, ye shall be free indeed" (KJV)

I CONFESS ⧸
I am free. Satan is trying to attack me, but I praise You, Lord, for sickness and disease have no right in my life. I have been set free. Thank You, thank you, Lord. I am free. Lord, I speak life not death, and healing and health throughout my body and I ask it in the powerful name of Jesus. I know that it is done. Thank You, Lord!

📖 THE BIBLE DECLARES
John 10:10 "The thief cometh not, but for to steal, and to kill, and to destroy: I am come that they might have life, and that they might have it more abundantly."

I CONFESS ⧸
Lord, Satan has afflicted me with sickness and diseases but this is not your plan for my life. I am not sick, I am **redeemed**. **I am already healed**. I

take back what the Devil tried to steal. I am healthy. Lord, I speak life not death, and healing and health throughout my body and I ask it in the powerful name of Jesus. I know that it is done. Thank You, Lord! ✞

Carrie Harper Walton

Acts

📖 THE BIBLE DECLARES

Acts 5:16 "There came also a multitude out of the cities round about unto Jerusalem, bringing sick folks, and them which were vexed with unclean spirits: and they were healed everyone." (KJV)

I CONFESS ⸙

Satan, you have no power over me for you have no power over the Word. I have the Word. There is healing for all those that believe in the Word. Lord, I speak life not death, and healing and health throughout my body and I ask it in the powerful name of Jesus. I know that it is done. Thank You, Lord!

📖 THE BIBLE DECLARES

Acts 10:38 "How God anointed Jesus of Nazareth with the Holy Ghost and with power: who went about doing good, and healing all that were oppressed of the devil; for God was with him."

I CONFESS

I know that sickness is a tool of the Devil but I have been delivered. Lord, Your Word gives me power over Satan. He cannot put doubt in my mind. I know that I am healed. I thank You for assurance in Your Word Lord. Lord, I speak life not death, and healing and health throughout my body and I ask it in the powerful name of Jesus. I know that it is done. Thank You, Lord! ✟

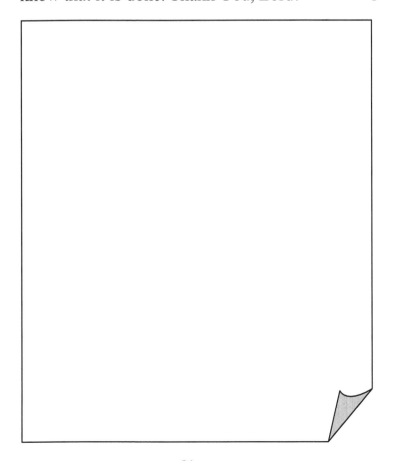

Romans

📖 THE BIBLE DECLARES

Rom. 4:17-21 "(As it is written, I have made thee a father of many nations,) before him whom he believed, even God, who quickeneth the dead, and calleth those things which be not as though they were. Who against hope believed in hope, that he might become the father of many nations, according to that which was spoken, So shall thy seed be.

And being not weak in faith, he considered not his own body now dead, when he was about an hundred years old, neither yet the deadness of Sara's womb: He staggered not at the promise of God through unbelief; but was strong in faith, giving glory to God; And being fully persuaded that, what he had promised, he was able also to perform." (KJV)

I CONFESS 🕿

I will never doubt Your Word, Lord, for I accept all your promises. Your Word gives me strength to hold on and to go forward. Lord, I speak life not death, and healing and health throughout my body and I ask it in the powerful name of Jesus. I know that it is done. Thank You, Lord!

📖 THE BIBLE DECLARES

Rom. 5:17 "For if by one man's offence death reigned by one; much more they which receive abundance of grace and of the gift of righteousness shall reign in life by one, Jesus Christ."

I CONFESS ⋦

Thank You, Lord, for living in me and making me whole. I know I am healed. I love You, Lord. I speak life not death, and healing and health throughout my body and I ask it in the powerful name of Jesus. I know that it is done. Thank You, Lord!

📖 THE BIBLE DECLARES

Rom. 8:11 "But if the Spirit of him that raised up Jesus from the dead dwell in you, he that raised up Christ from the dead shall also quicken your mortal bodies by his Spirit that dwelleth in you."

I CONFESS ⸱

I know this is my time in power with Christ in my life. I can feel Your presence, Your peace, and comfort in all that I am going through right now. I know I am victorious and I know, at this very moment, the Will of God is here for me. Lord, I speak life not death, and healing and health throughout my body and I ask it in the powerful name of Jesus. I know that it is done. Thank You, Lord!

📖 THE BIBLE DECLARES

Rom. 8:32 "He that spared not his own Son, but delivered him up for us all, how shall he not with him also freely give us all things?"

I CONFESS ⸱

Lord, I thank You for Your precious gift of the Holy Spirit that is living with me right now. Lord, I thank You for loving and caring for me. Even now, I know that Your spirit is healing me, creating a healthy and clean body. I thank You, Lord, because I know You care so much about me. Today, I know I can say I am healed only because You are the great **I AM THAT I AM (eimi—**

Strong's Concordance, G1510). I know my body is being healed of every suggestion of sickness and disease. Thank You, Lord, for I know that You have destroyed all sickness in my body. I speak life not death, and healing and health throughout my body and I ask it in the powerful name of Jesus. I know that it is done. Thank You, Lord!

📖 THE BIBLE DECLARES

Rom. 8:31 "What shall we then say to these things? If God be for us, who can be against us"

I CONFESS ⸲

God, I do not have to worry, for I know You are with me.

Satan, I know you keep trying but you are defeated.

Victory is mine. Lord, I speak Life not death, and healing and health throughout my body and I ask it in the powerful name of Jesus; I know that it is done. Thank You, Lord!

Carrie Harper Walton

📖 THE BIBLE DECLARES

Rom. 10:17 "So then faith cometh by hearing, and hearing by the word of God."

I CONFESS ⟨

Satan, I know what the Lord has done for me and you cannot stop me. I know that I am healed. I believe the Word, and that settles it, Devil.

Lord, I speak life not death, and healing and health throughout my body and I ask it in the powerful name of Jesus. I know that it is done. Thank You, Lord!   ✝

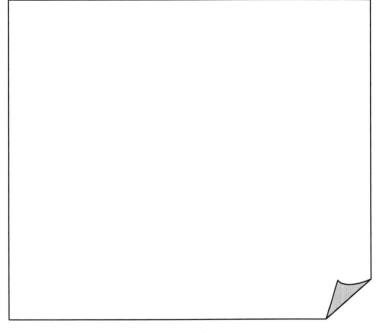

I Corinthians

📖 THE BIBLE DECLARES

1 Cor. 3:20-23 "And again, The Lord knoweth the thoughts of the wise, that they are vain. Therefore let no man glory in men. For all things are yours; Whether Paul, or Apollos, or Cephas, or the world, or life, or death, or things present, or things to come; all are yours; And ye are Christ's; and Christ is God's." (KJV)

I CONFESS ⸱

I thank You, Lord, for giving me all that I need to live a victorious life. Healing is mine and the Devil cannot touch it. Thank You, Lord, for my healing. I speak life not death, and healing and health throughout my body and I ask it in the powerful name of Jesus. I know that it is done. Thank You, Lord!

📖 THE BIBLE DECLARES

1 Cor. 6:15-17 "Know ye not that your bodies are the members of Christ? shall I then take the members of Christ, and make them the members of an harlot? God forbid.

What? know ye not that he which is joined to an harlot is one body? for two, saith he, shall be one flesh. But he that is joined unto the Lord is one spirit."

I CONFESS ⦃
I belong to God, from the top of my head to the soles of my feet. I belong to God, for I am washed in Jesus' precious blood. Lord, I speak life not death, and healing and health throughout my body and I ask it in the powerful name of Jesus. I know that it is done. Thank You, Lord!   ✠

II Corinthians

📖 THE BIBLE DECLARES

2 Cor. 10:4-5 "(For the weapons of our warfare are not carnal, but mighty through God to the pulling down of strong holds;) Casting down imaginations, and every high thing that exalteth itself against the knowledge of God, and bringing into captivity every thought to the obedience of Christ;" (KJV)

I CONFESS ⸰

Your Word, Lord, is sure and pure. Lord, I know Your Word is power. Nothing can ever stand up to God's Word. All evil will bow to the name Jesus Christ. Lord, I speak life not death, and healing and health throughout my body and I ask it in the powerful name of Jesus. I know that it is done. Thank You!

📖 THE BIBLE DECLARES

2 Cor. 3:17 "Now the Lord is that Spirit: and where the Spirit of the Lord is, there is liberty."

I CONFESS ⌇

Thank you, Lord, for coming within my life and saving me. I am free from bondage. I belong to You. I praise and Worship You, Lord. I speak life not death, and healing and health throughout my body and I ask it in the powerful name of Jesus. I know that it is done. Thank You, Lord!

📖 THE BIBLE DECLARES

2 Cor. 10:4-5 "(For the weapons of our warfare are not carnal, but mighty through God to the pulling down of strong holds;) Casting down imaginations, and every high thing that exalteth itself against the knowledge of God, and bringing into captivity every thought to the obedience of Christ;"

I CONFESS ⌇

Lord, I keep Your Words before my eyes and Your promises in my heart. **I am already healed!!!** Lord, I speak life not death, and healing and health throughout my body and I ask it in the powerful name of Jesus. I know that it is done. Thank You, Lord.   ✞

Galatians

📖 THE BIBLE DECLARES

Gal. 3:13-14 "Christ hath redeemed us from the curse of the law, being made a curse for us: for it is written, Cursed is every one that hangeth on a tree: That the blessing of Abraham might come on the Gentiles through Jesus Christ; that we might receive the promise of the Spirit through faith." (KJV)

I CONFESS ⟨

Lord, I am blessed and I thank You for loving me unconditionally. I thank You, for I have received all my promises according to the Word. Lord, I speak life not death, and healing and health throughout my body and I ask it in the powerful name of Jesus. I know that it is done. Thank You, Lord! ✝

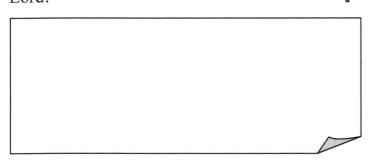

Carrie Harper Walton

Phillipians

📖 THE BIBLE DECLARES

Phil. 4:6-7 "Be careful for nothing; but in everything by prayer and supplication with thanksgiving let your requests be made known unto God. And the peace of God, which passeth all understanding, shall keep your hearts and minds through Christ Jesus." (KJV)

I CONFESS ▰

Lord, I seek Your presence and I take peace and comfort in knowing You will hear my cry. Thank You for listening to me. Lord, I speak life not death, and healing and health throughout my body and I ask it in the powerful name of Jesus. I know that it is done. I Thank You, Lord! ☨

Colossians

📖 THE BIBLE DECLARES

Col 1:12 "Giving thanks unto the Father, which hath made us meet to be partakers of the inheritance of the saints in light: Who hath delivered us from the power of darkness, and hath translated us into the kingdom of his dear Son:" (KJV)

I CONFESS ⸱

Lord, I thank You for my deliverance. I know that in You there is no sickness and Your Word declares that I am healed. Lord, I speak life not death, and healing and health throughout my body and I ask it in the powerful name of Jesus. I know that it is done. Thank You, Lord!　　　✝

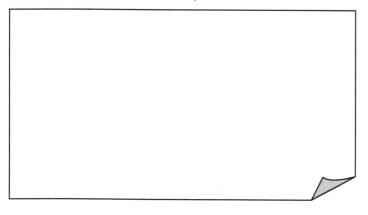

I Thessalonians

📖 THE BIBLE DECLARES

1 Thess. 5:23 "And the very God of peace sanctify you wholly; and I pray God your whole spirit and soul and body be preserved blameless unto the coming of our Lord Jesus Christ." (KJV)

I CONFESS ☙

Lord, I know that I am complete in you because You died for me. I can declare power in Your name and in Your Word. Lord, I speak life not death, and healing and health throughout my body and I ask it in the powerful name of Jesus. I know that it is done. Thank You, Lord! ✟

II TIMOTHY

📖 THE BIBLE DECLARES

2 Tim. 1:7 "For God hath not given us the spirit of fear; but of power, and of love, and of a sound mind." (KJV)

I CONFESS

Satan, I do not care what you may try to do to me, for I have no fear of you. I am set free because of perfect love. I do not fear, and because of His Word, I have a sound mind and my spirit is at peace.

Lord, I speak life not death, and healing and health throughout my body and I ask it in the powerful name of Jesus. I know that it is done. Thank You, Lord!

📖 THE BIBLE DECLARES

2 Tim 3:16-17 "All scripture is given by inspiration of God, and is profitable for doctrine, for reproof, for correction, for instruction in righteousness: That the man of God may be perfect, throughly furnished unto all good works."

I CONFESS ⸙

Lord, I thank You for the *Holy Bible*, for it is ointment to all my scratches. Lord, when I apply it, I am immediately healed. Thank You for the medicine. Lord, I speak life not death, and healing and health throughout my body and I ask it in the powerful name of Jesus. I know that it is done. Thank You, Lord! ✚

Hebrews

📖 THE BIBLE DECLARES

Heb. 10:23 "Let us hold fast the profession of our faith without wavering; (for he is faithful that promised;" (KJV)

I CONFESS ⸱

God, your Word is sure and I must cling to my faith in it. I know You will honor Your promises. Lord, I speak life not death, and healing and health throughout my body and I ask it in the powerful name of Jesus. I know that it is done. Thank You, Lord!

📖 THE BIBLE DECLARES

Heb. 10:35-36 "Cast not away therefore your confidence, which hath great recompence of reward. For ye have need of patience, that, after ye have done the will of God, ye might receive the promise".

I CONFESS ⸱

Lord, I seek Your will, let Your will become mine. Your will is found in your Word. Lord, I speak life not death, and healing and health throughout my body and I ask it in the powerful name of Jesus. I know that it is done. Thank You, Lord!

THE BIBLE DECLARES

Heb. 12:12-13 "Wherefore lift up the hands which hang down, and the feeble knees; And make straight paths for your feet, lest that which is lame be turned out of the way; but let it rather be healed."

I CONFESS

Lord, I thank You for Your promises. They are mine, now. I dwell on the promises not the problems in the world. I know I am experiencing healing in my body. I am happy and rejoice every time I think of Your Word. Lord, I speak life not death, and healing and health throughout my body and I ask it in the powerful name of Jesus. I know that it is done. Thank You, Lord!

THE BIBLE DECLARES

Heb. 13:20-21 "Now the God of peace, that brought again from the dead our Lord Jesus, that great shepherd of the sheep, through the blood of the everlasting covenant, Make you perfect in every good work to do his will, working in you that which is well pleasing in his sight, through Jesus Christ; to whom be glory forever and ever. Amen"

I CONFESS ≶

Lord, I know You have a plan for my life. I pray and receive it. Lord, I speak life not death, and healing and health throughout my body and I ask it in the powerful name of Jesus. I know that it is done. Thank You, Lord! ♱

James

📖 THE BIBLE DECLARES

Jas. 5:14-15 "Is any sick among you? Let him call for the elders of the church; and let them pray over him, anointing him with oil in the name of the Lord: And the prayer of faith shall save the sick, and the Lord shall raise him up; and if he have committed sins, they shall be forgiven him." (KJV)

I CONFESS ᛒ

Lord, I must pray in faith knowing healing is taking control over my body. I receive my healing. Lord, I speak life not death, and healing and health throughout my body and I ask it in the powerful name of Jesus. I know that it is done. Thank You, Lord! ✝

I Peter

📖 THE BIBLE DECLARES

1 Pet. 2:24 "Who his own self bare our sins in his own body on the tree, that we, being dead to sins, should live unto righteousness: by whose stripes ye were healed." (KJV)

I CONFESS

The Word of God tells me that I do not have to wait for my healing. **I am already healed**. It happened on Calvary's cross. Jesus Christ paid the ultimate price, dying for my sins. Lord, I speak life not death, and healing and health throughout my body and I ask it in the powerful name of Jesus. I know that it is done. Thank You, Lord! ✞

Carrie Harper Walton

II Peter

📖 THE BIBLE DECLARES

2 Pet. 1:3-4 "According as his divine power hath given unto us all things that pertain unto life and godliness, through the knowledge of him that hath called us to glory and virtue: Whereby are given unto us exceeding great and precious promises: that by these ye might be partakers of the divine nature, having escaped the corruption that is in the world through lust." (KJV)

I CONFESS ≋

My healing is based on God's Word. I have complete health and wealth in Jesus Christ. I thank You for my healing. I speak life not death, and healing and health throughout my body and I ask it in the powerful name of Jesus. I know that it is done. Thank You, Lord! ✞

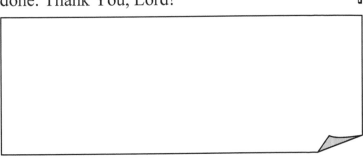

I John

📖 THE BIBLE DECLARES
1 John 3:8 "He that committeth sin is of the devil; for the devil sinneth from the beginning. For this purpose the Son of God was manifested, that he might destroy the works of the devil." (KJV)

I CONFESS
Satan, I know your works, but the Word of God is clear; you have no power or right to touch my body. Sickness and Disease, you have no legal right to my body because I am a child of God.

Lord, I speak life not death, and healing and health throughout my body and I ask it in the powerful name of Jesus. I know that it is done. Thank You, Lord!

📖 THE BIBLE DECLARES
1 John 3:21-22 "Beloved, if our hearts condemn us not, then have we confidence toward God. And, whatsoever we ask, we receive of him, because we keep his commandments, and do those things that are pleasing in his sight."

I CONFESS ⧢

I believe in the Word of God with **all** my soul.
Lord, I know You expect me to keep Your
commandments and I write them on my heart.
Lord, I speak life not death, and healing and health
throughout my body and I ask it in the powerful
name of Jesus. I know that it is done. Thank You,
Lord!

 THE BIBLE DECLARES

1 John 4:4 "Ye are of God, little children, and have
overcome them: because greater is he that is in
you, than he that is in the world"

I CONFESS ⧢

Lord, I have overcome things of this world and I
stand on Your Word. Your Word is true in my life
and I thank You for the *Holy Bible*. Lord, I speak
life not death, and healing and health throughout
my body and I ask it in the powerful name of
Jesus. I know that it is done. Thank You, Lord.

📖 THE BIBLE DECLARES

1 John 5:4 "For whatsoever is born of God over cometh the world: and this is the victory that overcometh the world, even our faith."

I CONFESS ₹

Lord, I will not let the cares of this world overshadow me. Sickness and disease are not of God, and by faith, I claim victory. Lord, I speak life not death, and healing and health throughout my body and I ask it in the powerful name of Jesus. I know that it is done. Thank You, Lord!

📖 THE BIBLE DECLARES

1 John 5:14-15 "And this is the confidence that we have in him, that, if we ask any thing according to his will, he heareth us: And if we know that he hear us, whatsoever we ask, we know that we have the petitions that we desired of him."

I CONFESS ₹

Lord, Your Word contains Your will. I have confidence that if I ask for healing, and if it is Your Will, You will not withhold it from me. I believe You hear me and I thank You for listening.

Lord, I speak life not death, and healing and health throughout my body and I ask it in the powerful name of Jesus. I know that it is done. Thank You, Lord! ✞

III John

📖 THE BIBLE DECLARES

3 John 2 "Beloved, I wish above all things that thou mayest prosper and be in health, even as thy soul prospereth." (KJV)

I CONFESS ≶

Lord, You alone have provided all of my needs. In You, I trust. Thank You, Lord. I know You are working Your will in my life. I turn over the control of my life to You. Lord, I speak life not death, and healing and health throughout my body and I ask it in the powerful name of Jesus. I know that it is done, Thank You, Lord! ✟

Revelation

📖 THE BIBLE DECLARES

Rev. 12:11 "And they overcame him by the blood of the Lamb, and by the word of their testimony; and they loved not their lives unto the death." (KJV)

I CONFESS ⟨

Lord, my healing proves that I overcame the surge of Satan in my life. I will take every opportunity to testify of Your goodness and faithfulness. I gladly testify of Your awesomeness, Lord. I pray my testimony will help build faith in someone else I meet along the way. I pray they will come to the Lord through His Word. They will realize healing is theirs by speaking the Word. Lord, I speak life not death, and healing and health throughout my body and I ask it in the powerful name of Jesus. I know that it is done. Thank You, Lord! ✟

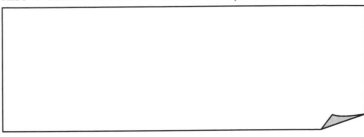

Let Us Pray

 Oh, Father God, thank You for the precious, powerful promises found in the *Healing Scriptures*. Father, I confess and declare that I receive Your Word and I thank You for all that You have done and shown to me. I thank You for loving me so much and giving Your life for me. As I seek closeness to You, I see Your Word more clearly. I realize that Satan has no power over me. I let him know, that he is not a lion, he is an impostor and I thank You for the power You have given me over the Devil.

Lord, we do as You admonish us, each time we face a crisis we pray for Your guidance and protection. As we come to the completion of this book we come acknowledging You. We ask for a special blessing upon the readers of this book. Let Your healing virtue flow throughout their bodies; healing, and strengthening.

Oh, Father, as I can feel Your presence, let those reading this book also feel Your presence in their lives. Starting today, may those people that are

Carrie Harper Walton

sick in body, mind, or spirit, keep Your Word
written in their hearts.

According to Your Word, "if two of you shall
agree on earth as touching anything that they shall
ask, it shall be done for them of my Father which
is in heaven (Matt 18:19)."

Thus, we claim in each of our lives, that You have
declared, **"You are already HEALED!!!"**

AMEN and AMEN and AMEN!!!   ✞

Do You Know Christ as Your Personal Savior?

Do you know that God loves you?

I would be remiss if I did not tell you that if you do not know Christ as your personal Savior, you are missing out on the best thing you could ever have. When someone has a personal relationship with Christ, the *Healing Scriptures* are more powerful.

The *Holy Bible* tells us that, "For God so loved the world, that he gave his only begotten Son, that whosoever believeth in him should not perish, but have everlasting life (John 3:16)."

It does not matter if we have said and done things that were wrong (sinned) the *Holy Bible* tells us that "For all have sinned, and come short of the glory of God; (Romans 3:23)." We must realize, because God is perfect and holy, that sin separates us from Him. The bible goes on to tell us that "the wages of sin is death (Romans 6:23a)."

Carrie Harper Walton

Over 2000 years ago, God sent his son, Jesus, to earth to die for our sins.

Jesus paid the penalty for your sins. This was God's demonstration of His love for us.

God wants you to become His child. You can **choose** to ask Jesus to enter your life and forgive your sins.

If You want to accept Christ as Your Savior and turn from sin. You can ask Him to be your Lord and Savior by repeating this simple prayer with me.

Lord Jesus, I believe You are the Son of God. Thank you for dying on the cross for my sins. I repent and turn away from sin. Please forgive my sins and give me the gift of eternal life. I ask You to come into my life and my heart and to be my Lord and Savior. My desire is to serve You. Amen.

Mem# 3637/6741

B.L. 786-326-5596

zip 33023

#844-309-5445

Made in the USA
Lexington, KY
09 August 2012